STAY ON TOP

Building a Life
That Never Falls Apart

BY LARRY HUTTON

Harrison House
Tulsa, OK

Stay on Top: Building A Life That Never Falls Apart
Copyright © 2010 by Larry Hutton
P. O. Box 822
Broken Arrow, OK 74013-0822

Published by Harrison House
Tulsa, OK 74145
www.harrisonhouse.com
ISBN: 978-160683-654-5

Editors: Grady King, Steve Rankin, Larry Hutton

CONTENTS

ACKNOWLEDGEMENTS

Liz, thank you so much for staying faithful to the call of God on our lives. I'm so thankful for you. God has truly given me the best when He gave me you!

Rachel, you have brought so much joy into our family. You've turned into a beautiful young woman of God. Keep that tender heart that you've always had, and the Lord will take you far in life. You are truly my princess!

David Wirginis and Jeremiah Harris, two of the best employee's one could ever hope for! Your dedication and unwavering love for both us and the ministry is truly admirable. Thank you both so much for all the extra hours you put in for the Lord. It does not go unnoticed on earth or in heaven. Crowns and rewards are being laid up for you!

Partners of LHM, your faithfulness and loyalty are appreciated more than words can express. Your continued financial support has enabled us to minister to the multitudes! Thank you for being co-laborers with us. Your rewards will be great!

DEDICATION

I dedicate this book to two very special people.

First of all, I want to thank my Mom, Betty Ann Hutton. Thank you for always being there for me and the family. I admire your teachable spirit and your dedication to the Lord. You are more of an example after which people can pattern their lives than you will ever know!

There are many things that I could thank you for, but there are two things that really stand out. You always taught me that if something is worth doing, it is worth doing right! That helped put a spirit of excellence in me. You also always told me that I could do anything that I put my mind to. You instilled a no-quit mentality in me.

I will be forever and eternally grateful that God used you to help make me what I am today!

Second, I want to thank my close friend Pastor Dan Coflin. Even though we grew up together and knew each other in elementary school, it was in 1976 that God used you in a mighty way to impact my life! Thank you for pouring the Word of God into me, and spending so much time discipling me. I know that the multitudes that God has touched through this ministry will be credited to your account. I love you, thank God continually for you, and am honored to call you friend!

INTRODUCTION

How would you like to live the rest of your life without falling? No more falling into sin. No more falling into depression. No more falling into helplessness. No more falling into despair. No more falling into misery. No more falling into strife. No more falling into man's traps, scams, or snares that are designed to deceive and hurt you. No more falling period!

God does not want us falling into any curse from which He has already redeemed us. Jesus paid an awesome price for us, enabling us to walk in victory, not defeat. He didn't provide redemption for us just "part of the time." Redemption is continually available to us.

Second Corinthians 1:10 says, *"Who (God) delivered us from so great a death, and doth deliver: in whom we trust that he will yet deliver us" (emphasis mine).*

God's deliverance is ongoing, progressive, never-ending, and always available. We are redeemed from sin, fear, sickness and disease, emotional problems, poverty and lack, sleep disorders, broken hearts, unforgiveness, and every other curse that could be listed. And according to God, we don't have to *fall* into any curse!

So, if you want to position yourself so that you *never fall again*, then get ready. The revelation from God's Word shared in this book will enable you to do just that!

CHAPTER ONE

THE POWER OF SEVEN

Is it possible to go through the rest of our lives on earth without falling? Though it may sound like an impossible feat, we must remember that with God all things are possible! Let's see what God has to say about the subject. Look at Jude, verse 24.

> **Now unto Him that is able to <u>keep you from falling</u>, and to present *you* faultless before the presence of His glory with exceeding joy.**

This verse doesn't say that God is able to keep us from falling "sometimes" or "most of the time." No! God is able to keep us from falling—all the time!

Jude 24 says that God is able to keep us from falling. There are a couple of things I want you to see here. First of all, since it says that God is able to keep us from *falling*, then there must be "attacks" that are going to come against us in our lives—attacks specifically designed to make us fall. Obviously, God is not the one sending them. Remember, He's the one who desires to *keep us from falling*. It is our enemy who wants us to fall, not God!

In numerous scriptures we are warned that every one of us will encounter problems, situations, and circumstances in this life that will attempt to knock us down. However, the second thing I want you to see is that no matter what attack comes our way, God is able to keep us from falling!

Jesus talked about these "attacks" in John 16:33. In the first part of the verse, He tells us that when we're in Him, then we will have His supernatural peace. Then, in the middle of the verse, He tells us what to expect as long as we are living on the earth. He said, *"In the world ye shall have tribulation."* The Greek word for tribulation speaks of emotional problems, stress, pressure, persecution, and hardships. This is telling us that we all will face difficulties in this life. There is no way around it!

Don't let that statement get you down because Jesus didn't say "You are going to have tribulation, so just learn to live with it." No! After He told us that all of us are going to face tests and trials, He went on to say, *"But be of good cheer; I have overcome the world."*

In other words, Jesus has already defeated every problem that you will face, every curse that is arrayed against you, and every situation that is designed to knock you down. And since He has given you His peace, you can live in His peace right in the midst of every storm!

The end of that verse quoted from the Amplified Bible says that he has, *"...deprived it* [the world] *of power to harm you and conquered it for you."* So, that means the world's "power" or "ability" to harm us has already been removed. And when did Jesus do that? He did it when He was on the cross!

Let me say it another way. When a test or trial that is designed to knock you down comes against you, Jesus has already faced it at the cross and has taken its "ability" to knock you down away! So when any test or trial comes your way, it has already had the power or ability to overcome you extracted. When you know you have God and His ability in you, then you can understand why the scripture says *"God is able to keep you from falling."* You can start rejoicing right now! Why? Because He has already defeated the enemy for you. Now that is something you can get excited about!

Since Jude says that God is able to keep us from falling, there must be a way for us to tap into that ability. There must be things we can do to prevent ourselves from falling. Let's look at another verse. Let's read 2 Peter, chapter 1, verse 10.

Wherefore the rather, brethren, give diligence to make your calling and election sure: for if ye do these things, ye shall <u>never fall</u>.

Did you see what God said? He said if we do *"these things"* we shall *"never fall."* What does *never* mean? The Greek word means *certainly not, by no means, not at all, never.* In other words, if we do the *things* that God is referring to, then we will never fall—*certainly not, by no means, not at all*! I like that! This verse is informing us that we can live a life of victory. God wants His children to overcome, rule, and reign in life.

Let's find out what we have to do in order for God to *keep us from falling*. Let's look at the verses leading up to verse ten, starting with verse five.

And beside this, giving all diligence, add to your faith virtue; and to virtue knowledge; and to knowledge temperance; and to temperance patience; and to patience godliness; and to godliness brotherly kindness; and to brotherly kindness charity. For if <u>these things</u> be in you, and abound, they make you that you shall neither be barren nor unfruitful in the knowledge of our Lord Jesus Christ. But he that lacks <u>these things</u> is blind, and cannot see afar off, and hath forgotten that he was purged from his old sins. Wherefore the rather, brethren, give diligence to make your calling and election sure: for <u>if you do these things, ye shall never fall</u>.

When verses eight, nine, and ten say *"these things,"* they are all referring to the things God listed in verses five through seven. So let's look at them.

First let me briefly summarize verses one through four of 2 Peter Chapter 1. In those verses, the Word tells us that if we will acquire a precise and correct knowledge of God, then His favor and prosperity will be multiplied to us in every realm (spiritual, physical, financial, mental, and emotional). That knowledge will enable us to live Godly lives and help us to receive all the abundant resources God has already provided for us through His power. As we apply that knowledge, all of God's wonderful promises will become realities in our lives and then we will find ourselves walking in the divine characteristics of

God himself.

Then, in verse five, it tells us that we need to be diligent to *"add to our faith."* Filling ourselves with the knowledge of God builds up our faith; however, verse five tells us that we need more than just faith to keep from falling. In fact, God lists seven things that we need to be diligent about in our lives. Remember, if we do *"these things,"* we will never fall!

I will list the seven things, as well as define them for you. We will then discuss them in detail in the following chapters.

1. Virtue - a virtuous course of thought, feeling, and action. Moral excellence, modesty and purity

2. Knowledge - understanding God's Word

3. Temperance - self-control

4. Patience - steadfastness, constancy and endurance

5. Godliness - reverence and respect

6. Brotherly kindness - loving your brothers and sisters in Christ

7. Charity - love, affection, good will and benevolence

After God lists these seven things, He tells us in the next verse (verse eight) that if the above things are increasing in our lives, our lives will be fertile and fruitful. Then verse ten tells us that if we do *those things*, we will never fall!

Someone may believe or say, "Brother, you know

that it's not possible for us to *never* fall. After all, we're human." Yes, we are human. But we have the Greater One living on the inside of us—and that's what makes impossibilities possible! (See Mark 9:23.) I believe that what God says is truth. He cannot tell a lie. So, if we do the things listed since He says the result will be that "we will never fall" and God cannot lie—it has to be possible.

God is not an unjust or unfair God. If we were not able to do these things, it would be unjust and unfair for Him to tell us to do them. However, since God is just and fair, we know that *we can* do everything that God has listed. We can do all things (including the ones listed in 2 Peter 1) through Christ who strengthens us. And when we do, then we can expect Him to *"keep us from falling."*

These verses list seven things that we need to be diligent about in our lives. God told us that diligence in these areas will keep us from falling into the troubles that we will face in this life. That means we don't have to fall into the traps that the enemy has laid out for us. In fact, God went so far as to say that we will *never fall* if we do what this passage tells us. That's a remarkable statement! Meditate on that for just a moment. Think about never falling into sin again, never falling into depression again, never falling into offenses again, never falling into worry again, and never falling into fear again. Listen, since God said it is possible- it is possible!

That does not mean we are never going to encounter those things. It just means that we don't have to "fall" as prey to them. There are attacks we will all face that are meant to knock us down, and keep us down. However, our God, who is rich in mercy, will keep us from being knocked down when we add these seven things to our faith. According to God, we can add these seven things to our faith, and then be able to overcome every test and trial that comes our way!

The Greek word for add means; *to supply, to furnish, to present.* It also means; *to be assisted.* So, in essence, the word means *to assist by furnishing and supplying.*

When God says to "add" these things to our faith, He is letting us know that they are *assistants* to our faith, *furnishing* us with all the *supplies* we need to live a victorious life. As we study these seven things, let's recognize them as "assistants."

CHAPTER TWO

VIRTUE

In Second Peter, chapter 1, verses 5-7, God gives us a list of seven "assistants" that we need to use with our faith in order to live a victorious life.

The first assistant He instructs us to add to our faith is "*virtue.*" As a reminder, the Greek word for *virtue* means *a virtuous course of thought, feeling, and action.* It also means *moral goodness, moral excellence, modesty, and purity.* So, when God tells us to support our faith with "*virtue,*" He is in essence telling us that our thoughts, feelings, and actions are supposed to be modest, pure, and morally excellent. Simply stated, it means that we are to control our thoughts and feelings so that we act in line with God's Word.

Our thoughts control our feelings, and our feelings control our actions. Therefore, to build the foundation of *virtue* we must fill our minds with God's Word so that we think *God's thoughts.* When our minds are renewed to continually think the way that God thinks, then we will control our feelings and our actions. Subsequently, our thoughts, feelings, and actions will be morally good, modest, and pure.

Notice, one of the definitions of *virtue* is *moral excellence*. Here is a list of synonyms for the word *moral*. As you read them, make a decision that *this is how you are going to think, feel and act*. Synonyms for *moral* include: Ethical, good, right, honest, decent, proper, honorable, fair, just, principled, respectable, praiseworthy, admirable, and trustworthy.

Not only do we need to make sure our thoughts, feelings, and actions toward others are good and pure, we must also learn to think all of these things about ourselves as well! What are your *thoughts, feelings, and actions* with regard to yourself? Do you continually think or say things like, "I'm so stupid" or, "I can never do anything right" or, "I'm such a mess"? Thoughts like those will not keep you from falling—*they will cause you to fall!* You must train yourself to think virtuous thoughts like, *I am a good person. I do things right. I'm an honest person. I'm fair to people. I am respectable. I am admirable. People can trust me.*

Someone might say, "*I don't want to say those things about myself. That would be prideful. After all, the Bible tells us not to think highly of ourselves.*" Actually, the contrary is true. The Bible tells you to think of yourself highly.

Look at Romans 12:3. It tells us that a child of God is not to think of himself *"more highly than he ought."* God didn't say "Don't think of yourself highly." He said *"more"* highly. A closer study will reveal that we are actually supposed to think highly of ourselves.

The Greek word for *highly* means what is *proper*. So, the question becomes, "What is proper?" The answer is found in the verse. God said that a man is not to think of himself more highly *"than he ought."* The phrase *"than he ought"* comes from a Greek word which means *what is necessary*. Subsequently, the Greek gives the meaning of *"necessary."* Let's look at the definition very closely.

1A necessity lying in the nature of the case.

1B necessity brought on by circumstances or by the conduct of others toward us.

1C necessity in reference to what is required to attain some end.

1D necessity of law and command, of duty.

1E necessity established by the counsel and decree of God.[1]

What is necessary depends on the *nature of the case.* It depends on the *circumstance or the conduct of others toward us.* It depends on *what is required to attain some end.* It depends on what we've been *commanded* to do. And finally, it depends on the *established counsel and decree of God*—i.e. what He has said in His Word!

These things can be used to determine what is proper when thinking about ourselves. We must look at each situation separately, assess the actions of others toward us, determine what is required to attain a goal, always fulfill our duties, and obey God and His Word.

Look at Jesus for an example. In some cases, He spoke of Himself as the Light of the World and the Son of God. He told people He was anointed. He told people to follow Him. He spoke to religious leaders and called them snakes and vipers. He drove out the money changers from the temple. He forgave sin, healed the sick, raised the dead, and brought deliverance to the captives.

Conversely, on other occasions He "opened not His mouth," hid His whereabouts, and escaped when the rulers wanted to kill Him. When Peter was being controlled by Satan, He rebuked him. When Judas was being controlled by Satan, He didn't resist him. He did mighty miracles in Capernaum, but only healed a few in Nazareth. In some situations, He was bold as a lion. In others, He was quiet and subdued.

Was Jesus having wavering thoughts about Himself in these different situations? Was He thinking highly in some cases and lowly in others? Absolutely not! He was actually thinking what was proper, and He was thinking "soberly."

That's what the verse here in Romans goes on to say. It says to think "soberly, according as God hath dealt to every man the measure of faith." The word "soberly" means to be of sound mind or sane. Figuratively it means moderate. That's the way Jesus was. Jesus was always sound-minded but moderate. However, He always thought of Himself highly.

His words and actions depended on the nature of the case and the circumstance or the conduct of others toward Him. He did what was required to attain some end, and what He was commanded to do. Everything Jesus said and did was based on the established counsel and decree of God. In every situation Jesus knew who he was, what he would do, and where He was going! Every thought and action of His was in line with the will of God for His life.

That is what is meant in Romans 12:3 when God tells every Christian not to "think of himself more highly than he ought to think, but to think soberly according as God hath dealt to every man the measure of faith." Jesus leaned upon His faith in God, and then only said what He heard God say, and did what He saw His Father do. He used virtue as an assistant to His faith—and God kept Him from falling!

We are supposed to think of ourselves in the same way Jesus did! Philippians 2:5 says, "Let this mind be in you, which was also in Christ Jesus."

Remember, virtue means a virtuous course of thought, feeling, and action. Thinking correctly about others, as well as ourselves, is a very important virtue. If we learn to get those thoughts lined up with God's Word, we're on the right course. And when we get on that course, God will keep us from falling!

CHAPTER THREE

KNOWLEDGE

G od gave us a list of seven things that we need
to add to our faith. He told us that diligence in
these areas will keep us from falling into the traps and
pitfalls that we will face in this life. There are attacks that
are going to come our way that are meant to knock
us down and keep us down. But God, who is rich in
mercy, will keep us from being knocked down when we
add these seven things to our faith.

We discovered that the first assistant He instructed
us to add to our faith was *virtue*. As a reminder, the
Greek word for *virtue* means *a virtuous course of thought,
feeling and action*. It also means *moral goodness, moral
excellence, modesty and purity*. We have to train ourselves
to think, feel, and act with excellence, modesty, and
purity—toward ourselves as well as others. Remember,
our thoughts control our feelings and our feelings control our actions. Therefore, to build the foundation of
virtue, we must fill our minds with God's Word so that
we think *God's thoughts*. When our minds are renewed

to continually think the way that God thinks, then we will control our feelings and our actions. Subsequently, our thoughts, feelings, and actions will be morally good, modest, and pure.

Now let's discuss the second assistant. God said to add to virtue, *"knowledge."* The Greek word used for *knowledge* speaks of a deeper understanding of God's Word. In fact, this Greek word comes from another Greek word which is used by the Jews to express the act of sexual intercourse between a man and a woman. This shows us that the knowledge God is speaking of here is not a casual one, but rather an intimate one.

We find this same Greek word used in John 8:32. Verses 31-32 say, *"If ye continue in my word, then are ye my disciples indeed. And ye shall <u>know</u> the truth, and the truth shall make you free."* It is not a casual knowledge of the truth that will bring freedom into our lives. We must have a close, personal, and thorough knowledge of God's Word in order to walk in the liberty that God has provided for us.

Look at verse 31 again. It says, *"If ye <u>continue</u> in my word..."* The word *continue* means *to stay, abide, dwell, or remain.* Here's a good example: If a parent tells a child, "If you stay right here and don't move from that spot until I tell you to, I'm going to give you a gift." I guarantee you, that child knows (without any further explanation) exactly what he must do if he wants that gift. That's what God is telling us in these two verses. "Just stay put in My Word. Live in it. Remain right there! Then I'll cause your *knower* to be enlightened, and you will experience freedom in every area of your life!"

In order to get this kind of knowledge working for us, we must spend time reading, meditating, and speaking God's Word. I'm reminded of what the Apostle James said in James 1:25. I'll quote it from the Amplified Bible.

But he who looks carefully into the faultless law, the [law] of liberty, and is faithful to it *and* perseveres in looking into it, being not a heedless listener who forgets but an active doer [who obeys], he shall be blessed in his doing (his life of obedience).

The kind of knowledge that will keep you from falling must be sought after! Colossians 2:3 tells us that in Christ *"are hid all the treasures of wisdom and knowledge."* Notice the knowledge that we need is "hid" in Christ. It's not hidden *from* us, it's hidden *for* us! Where is it hidden? In Christ! We are in Him aren't we? Then let's seek that knowledge.

Look at what God told Joshua (and us) in Joshua 1:8

This book of the law shall not depart out of thy mouth, but thou shalt meditate therein day and night, that thou mayest observe to do according to all that is written therein. For then thou shalt make thy way prosperous, and then thou shalt have good success.

Look at the New Living Translation.

Study this Book of Instruction continually. Meditate on it day and night so you will be sure to obey everything written in it. Only then will you prosper and succeed in all you do.

Do you want to keep yourself from falling? If you do, then you must aggressively go after this kind of knowledge.

Jesus said to *"seek first the kingdom of God and His righteousness"* (Matthew 6:33). He also said, *"Seek and ye shall find"* (Matthew 7:7). In Colossians 3:1, we're told to seek heavenly things, not earthly things. Hebrews 11:6 tells us that God *"is a rewarder of them that diligently seek Him."* Seek Him and you will be filled with His knowledge and well on your way to a victorious life!

CHAPTER FOUR

TEMPERANCE

Now let's discuss the third assistant that will help us to never fall. Second Peter 1:8 tells us that after we've added *knowledge*, then we need to add *"temperance."* The Greek word used here means *self control*. Strong's Concordance gives us further insight into this Greek word by giving us the meaning of self control. It says, *"The virtue of one who masters his desires and passions, especially his sensual appetites."*

A person who exercises self control is *one who masters his desires and passions, especially his sensual appetites.* Let me ask you some questions. And if you want temperance added to your life, then you must be *brutally honest* with yourself in answering them! Are there desires in your life that rule you? Do you have passions that control you? What sensual appetites dominate you?

Let me remind you of something the Apostle John said in 1 John 2:16.

For all that is in the world, the lust of the flesh, and the lust of the eyes, and the pride of life, is

not of the Father, but is of the world.

The *lust of the flesh,* the *lust of the eyes,* and the *pride of life* will attempt to drive, force, and coerce you. And if you don't control them, they <u>will</u> control you! What are some sensual appetites that try to *control us*? Someone might say, "Sexual lust." Yes, that is definitely something that would fall under *the lust of the flesh* and the *lust of the eyes,* but *sensual appetites* can include anything that feeds *any* of the senses. They can be things that you eat or drink that are not healthy for you. Do you yield to your flesh too often in eating or drinking those things?

What about the senses wanting to watch something on television or the Internet that you shouldn't be watching? Jesus is sitting right there with you and not enjoying it at all! There are also the ears that want to listen to ungodly music. Is the Holy Ghost in you enjoying that stuff getting down in your heart? Do you have a love of sports or other activities that drive you to miss church because you put them ahead of God? I told you that you must be brutally honest with yourself. Don't try to talk your way out of some of these things. Deal with them. It's the only way to add *temperance* to your life.

Now let me give you some really good news. YOU HAVE BEEN GIVEN SOME SUPERNATURAL EQUIPMENT. Remember the Greek word for *temperance* that we've been looking at? Well, the same Greek word is used in Galatians 5:23. Verses twenty-two and twenty-three list nine fruit of the Spirit that are inside the human spirit, once the Holy Spirit takes up residence inside a man. Verse twenty-three lists *temperance* as one of the fruit of the Spirit. It's the same Greek word that we've been discussing. It means *self control*.

Do you know what that means? It means God has given us *His self control* to use anytime we need it! It's not an "outside," natural self-control, where we have to do it on our own. It is an "inside," supernatural self-control. It has been given to us by God, and is at our disposal 24 hours a day, 7 days a week! Glory! We don't have to master our desires, passions, and sensual appetites by ourselves. We can *be strong in the Lord and in the power of His might* (Ephesians 6:10).

Now think about this: God said that we *can* add temperance to our faith. If He said that we can have this type of self control, then we can! We can stir up the fruit of the Spirit, called *temperance*, every time we get tempted or enticed. We do that by believing and speaking what God said. Tell yourself, "I'm not going to eat that, I'm not going to watch that, I'm not going to listen to that. I will not allow my flesh to control me—I'm in control!"

One really effective way to exercise *temperance* in your life is by prayer and fasting. If you want to hear your flesh scream, just try fasting! I've found in my own life that fasting not only has taught me to control my body, but also positioned me to hear from God.

So, since God has given us the fruit of temperance, let's add it to our repertoire. It is definitely going to help our faith and assist us in overcoming the obstacles of life!

CHAPTER FIVE

Patience

We've already discussed the first three assistants that God told us to add to our faith. Let's briefly review them. The first assistant He instructs us to add to our faith is *virtue*. In essence, *virtue* means that our thoughts, feelings, and actions are supposed to be modest, pure, and morally excellent. Simply stated, it means that we control our thoughts and feelings so that we act in line with God's Word.

The second assistant we are told to add to our faith is *knowledge*. This word means that we are to develop an *intimate* knowledge of God's Word. In order to be intimate with someone, you have to spend a lot of time with them and get to know them. That's what it takes to add this kind of knowledge to our faith.

The third assistant to our faith is *temperance*. This word means self-control. Strong's Concordance says that a person with self-control is one who "masters his desires and passions, especially his sensual appetites." We don't have to let our bodies, senses, or fleshly desires control us.

We also discovered that God has already given us *temperance* as part of the fruit of the Spirit. That means that we've been given supernatural equipment. We don't have to master our desires, passions and sensual appetites with our own strength. We can stir up this fruit of the Spirit called *temperance*, every time we get tempted or enticed. That means we don't have to fall into the temptations that come to us through the eyes or the flesh.

The next assistant that is mentioned in this passage of Scripture is *patience*. Most of the time in our English language, we use the word patience to mean *calm down and wait. Be tolerant and restrain yourself.*

Have you ever been in a hurry to get somewhere by car, but had someone in front of you driving extremely slowly, and you were unable to pass them? You may have found yourself getting edgy and had someone say to you, "Just be patient." What they meant was *restrain yourself, be tolerant, calm down, and just wait.* That is not what God meant when He instructed us to add *patience* to our repertoire.

The Greek word used here for *patience* is **hupomone**. It means endurance, perseverance, and steadfastness. It speaks of being strong in the midst of adversity, and refers to one who uses his faith to persevere and stand steadfast. In essence, this word speaks of the characteristics of a man who does not allow tests, trials, problems, or persecutions to force him away from his faith in God and His Word.

This Greek word is also used in Hebrews 12:1. We are told to run with "patience" the race that is set before us. Listen, when you run a race, you are not *waiting* to see if something is going to happen. No, your endurance, steadfastness, and perseverance *make* things happen. So, the first verse of Hebrews 12 tells us to run with endurance, steadfastness, and perseverance. But the second verse tells us where our attention is supposed to be while we run. It says,

Looking unto Jesus, the author and finisher of our faith; who for the joy that was set before him <u>endured</u> the cross.

The word *endured* is the Greek word **hupomeno**. It is the Greek word that the word **hupomone** (patience) comes from. **Hupomeno** means to endure, and to bear bravely and calmly. That's what Jesus did for us. When Jesus went to the cross, hung there and then died, He wasn't *waiting* to see how things were going to turn out. No, He persevered, remained steadfast to His purpose, and endured to the end. And when it was over, He rose victorious—and He did it all for us!

The reason we can exercise *patience* (endurance, steadfastness, and perseverance) is because of what Jesus did. He endured the cross. He paid the price. He defeated our enemies. He placed all principalities, powers, might, and dominion beneath our feet. Then He endued us with power from on high. He put His very life, nature, power, wisdom, and His ability on the inside of us. Wow! We are partakers of His divine nature! We have been made *overcomers* and are called *more than conquerors*. (See First John 5:4-5 and Romans 8:37.)

Jesus endured the cross, obtained the victory for us, and then told us to add patience to our faith. Therefore, when tests, trials, persecutions, hardships, and pressures come to us, we can *add* patience. We can endure, stand steadfast, and persevere.

Look at James 1:12: *"Blessed is the man who endureth temptation.* This word *endures* is the same word used when telling us that Jesus *endured* the cross. Notice, it says "blessed" is the man who endures. The opposite would also be true. "Cursed" is the man who does not persevere and remain steadfast when going through temptations. Thanks be unto our God, we can choose God's way and be blessed! *We can* endure, no matter what it looks like, feels like, or sounds like. Our Father cannot lie, and He said that we can add patience to our lives—therefore, we can!

Revelation 14:12 says, *"Here is the patience of the saints… they that keep the commandments of God, and the faith of Jesus."* I believe this verse gives us God's definition of *patience.* In essence, this verse says that a saint who exercises patience is one *who attends carefully to God's Word and remains faithful to Jesus!* That's definitely a person who ENDURES, STANDS STEADFAST AND PERSEVERES!

CHAPTER SIX

A PERFECT WORK

O ur study so far in 2 Peter 1:5-10 has revealed some wonderful truths. We found out that we don't have to fall into the traps that the enemy has laid out for us. In fact, God went so far as to say that we will *never fall* if we will do what this passage tells us. That's a remarkable statement! Meditate on that for just a moment. Think about never falling into sin again, never falling into depression again, never falling into offenses again, never falling into worry again, and never falling into fear again. And since God said it is possible, then it has to be possible!

Now that doesn't mean that we are never going to encounter those things again. It just means that we don't have to *fall* as prey to them. According to God, we can add these seven things to our faith, and then overcome every test and trial that comes our way!

We found out previously that these seven things are *assistants* to our faith. In order to establish them on the inside of you, I'm going to reiterate them throughout the book. The seven assistants God tells us to add to our faith (according to the King James Version) are *virtue, knowledge, temperance, patience, godliness, brotherly kindness,* and *charity.*

The first assistant is *virtue.* Virtue means modesty, purity, and moral excellence with regard to our thoughts, feelings, and actions. The second assistant is *knowledge.* Knowledge means a close, intimate understanding of God, which comes by being persistent in prayer and the study of His Word. The third assistant is *temperance.* Temperance means mastering our desires and passions, especially our sensual appetites—which really means, self-control. The fourth assistant is *patience.* Patience means endurance, perseverance, and steadfastness.

In the last chapter we discussed *patience* in some detail. We closed the teaching by quoting Revelation 14:12. That verse gives us some wonderful insight into what God meant when He used the Greek word **hupomone**, which is translated as *patience.* Let's look at it again. *"Here is the patience of the saints... they that keep the commandments of God, and the faith of Jesus."* Let me paraphrase that verse for you. *"Here is the endurance, perseverance and steadfastness of the saints... they are the ones who carefully attend to God's Word, and hold fast to their faith in Jesus and His Word."*

This kind of patience speaks of one who is strong in the midst of adversity, and also of one who uses his faith to persevere and stand steadfast. In essence, this word *patience* speaks of the characteristic of a man who does not allow tests, trials, problems, or persecutions to force him away from his faith in God or His Word. James uses this same Greek word in James, chapter one, verse four. Let's look at verses two through four.

My brethren, count it all joy when ye fall into divers [various] temptations; Knowing this, that the trying of your faith worketh patience. But let patience have her perfect work, that ye may be perfect and entire, wanting nothing.

Someone might say, "Hey, Brother Larry, that verse tells us to count it all joy <u>when</u> we fall into various temptations. I thought you said that we don't have to fall. That verse doesn't say <u>if</u> you fall, it says <u>when</u> you fall."

You're right, that's what it says. However, the word "fall" in this verse is a different Greek word than the one used in 2 Peter 1:10. In Peter, the word "fall" means *to stumble, to err, to make a mistake, to sin, to fall into misery, become wretched.* Here in James, the word "fall" means *to be encompassed.* If you are encompassed by something, then you are in the <u>midst of</u> or <u>surrounded by</u> it. In other words, this verse isn't saying that we are going to fall into defeat and failure. It is telling us to exercise the fruit of joy when we find ourselves *in the midst of or surrounded by* various tests and trials.

Let's take a close look at verse two. It tells us as brothers and sisters in Christ, to "count it all joy" when we find ourselves in the middle of adversity or when we're being enticed to sin. The words "count it" mean *to consider or think.* The word "joy" means *the cause or occasion of joy.*

Now, are you ready to shout? This verse is actually telling us that when we are being enticed to sin or when we find ourselves surrounded by adversity, we are supposed to think just as though we were in a situation that was bringing us great joy. Wow! That's just the opposite of what the world does. The world's system dictates that we act happy only when the circumstance or situation makes us happy. But God's system dictates that our joy is independent of our circumstances! Glory to God!

How is that possible? The next verse tells us. Look at verse three. *"Knowing this, that the trying of your faith worketh patience."* God starts the verse by saying, "Knowing this." He said that we are supposed to *know* that those tests and trials that come our way are trying to shake our faith. When we stir up joy, however, right in the middle of the storm, we engage our patience. That is, we strengthen our endurance, perseverance, and steadfastness.

Listen, these verses are letting us know that joy is a key ingredient to our patience (perseverance and steadfastness). When we stir up God's joy on the inside of us, it turns on a switch and allows His power to flow. Then we can stand steadfast, unmovable, and unshaken.

That reminds me of something the Prophet Nehemiah said. *"The joy of the Lord is your strength"* (Nehemiah 8:10). The Good News Translation says it this way, "The joy that the Lord gives you will make you strong." Well, if we are strong, then we are able to endure, persevere and stand steadfast.

James is letting us know that we do not have to fall or be defeated by adversity. It doesn't matter how big the adversity may appear. God has already said that we can add this type of patience to our faith and overcome *every* temptation that we encounter. In fact, the Apostle Paul had something to say about this very thing. Let's look at what he said. I believe it will help us tremendously.

Let me paraphrase what we read in James.

Brethren, when you find yourself being enticed to sin, or in the middle of adversity, stir up your inner joy (the joy of the Lord that is on the inside of you) and let that joy dominate you. Act just the same as you would if you were in a situation that was bringing you great joy. This will engage your patience, and help you stand firm in faith during the storm.

That's really good isn't it? We can use God's joy to help us exercise patience and stand strong in the midst of adversity!

Now, look at what Paul said in First Corinthians 10:13:

There has no temptation taken you but such as is common to man: but God is faithful, who will not suffer you to be tempted above that ye are able; but will with the temptation also make a way to escape, that ye may be able to bear it.

Listen, there isn't any test or trial that will come against us that is new or original. They are all "common to man." That means that all of them are things that many others have already faced and gone through.

It's a ploy of the devil to make us think that we are the

only ones going through what we're going through. No, not only are we not the only ones, but our God won't allow the adversity to be more than what we are capable of handling. In addition to that, our God is faithful and will make a way for us to break out and escape the adversity!

I asked the Lord, "Lord, if You don't allow us to be tested beyond our ability to escape and You also make a way for us to escape, then why are so many Christians falling when they face the adversities of life?" He answered, "They have no root system." Then He took me to the parable of the sower.

In Luke, chapter eight, it talks about a sower sowing seed. In verse six, it says that some of the seed fell upon a rock. The seed sprung up quickly, but then withered away because it lacked moisture. Then verse thirteen explains what verse six said.

They on the rock are they, which, when they hear, receive the word with joy; and these <u>have no root</u>, which for a while believe, and <u>in time of temptation fall away</u>.

There is no quick way to build a root system. It only occurs through constant prayer and meditation on the Word of God. When Christians don't mediate on the Word of God and fellowship with God in prayer on a regular basis, they'll do what the above verse says. They will believe for a while, but when the going gets tough, they'll speak doubt and act like they don't believe God's Word. Then, their doubt and unbelief will cause them to fall. Even the joy they had when they received the Word will no longer be apparent. Friends, this does not have to be the case!

We must water the seed of God's Word that is in us by continually meditating upon it and speaking it. This will cause our roots to shoot down deep, and then we will be able to stand strong in the midst of the storm. Hearing and meditating upon the Word will water the seeds of God's Word that have been planted in us. And when we plant and water God's Word, our Heavenly Father will make sure to bring forth the increase in our lives. (See First Corinthians 3:6.)

Now, let's go back to James 1:2-4 and look at the fourth verse. We've already seen, in verses two and three, we are supposed to use our faith to stir up joy when we encounter the troubles of life. Doing so will cause our steadfastness and endurance to be engaged. Now, let's look at the next verse.

But let patience have her perfect work, that ye may be perfect and entire, wanting nothing.

Wow, that sounds like a person who never falls! This passage tells us that through faith and steadfastness we will be become fully developed, with no lack or deficiency in any area of our lives. That doesn't sound like somebody who is falling and failing. It sounds like somebody who is standing and overcoming!

Let me close this chapter by paraphrasing this whole passage of Scripture.

Brethren, when you find yourself being enticed to sin, or in the middle of adversity, stir up your inner joy (the joy of the Lord that is on the inside of you), and let that joy dominate you. In other words, act just the same as you would if something had happened that made you really happy. This will engage your staying power, and help you stand firm in faith during the storm. And let your patience, that is, your endurance, perseverance and steadfastness, fully accomplish what it is meant to do. Then you will be fully developed, strong in character, lacking in nothing, and ready for anything and everything!

It's time to add this kind of patience to our faith, and we can!

CHAPTER SEVEN

GODLINESS

For learning purposes and to help strengthen your root system, let me reiterate the assistants we have studied so far.

The first assistant is *virtue*. Virtue means modesty, purity, and moral excellence with regards to our thoughts, feelings, and actions. The second assistant is *knowledge*. Knowledge means a close, intimate understanding of God that comes by spending time in prayer and in the study of His Word on a regular basis. The third assistant is *temperance*. Temperance means mastering our desires and passions, especially our sensual appetites. In other words, it means self-control. The fourth assistant is *patience*. Patience means endurance, perseverance, and steadfastness.

Now, let's go on to the fifth assistant. It is listed in 2 Peter 1:6. Look at verses five and six.

And beside this, giving all diligence, add to your faith virtue; and to virtue knowledge; And to

knowledge temperance; and to temperance patience; and to patience godliness.

God tells us to add *godliness* to our lives. The word *godliness* comes from the Greek word **eusebeia**. It is used fifteen times in the New Testament. It comes from two Greek words. The first is **eu**, which means *well*. The second is **sebomai**, which means *to be devout*. This speaks of an attitude of holiness and godliness. A person with this attitude is motivated to do only what is well-pleasing to God. He is faithful and steadfast, totally devoted to God and His ways.

It is interesting to note that the Apostle Paul used this word ten times, all of them being in his pastoral epistles, but it does not occur in his epistles to the churches. This reveals that those of us who are called into a pulpit ministry are to live our lives to the highest standard of godliness. Does that mean those who are not called to pulpit ministry don't have to live by the same standards? Absolutely not! It just means that those who are called to lead us are supposed to set the example for others to follow.

Paul told Timothy to, *be an example for the believers, in word, in conversation, in charity, in spirit and in purity (I Timothy 4:12)*. People whom God has called as leaders should be setting the example of how to live godly lives. Then, believers should pattern their lives after them.

If we want to add *godliness* to our lives, we must sell out to God! We must be *godly*. Doing so will affect what we watch on television, what movies we see, and how we talk to and treat others. Being godly will cause us to walk in love and forgiveness. It will also cause us to be tithers and givers—always putting God's Kingdom first with regards to our finances.

We are not talking about *works* of our own accord. We're talking about *works of righteousness*. Listen, if we are going to walk in godliness, it simply means that we are going to pattern our lives after God Himself! That means we're going to *act like God acts and talk like God talks.*

Ephesians 5:1 tells us to be an imitator of God. The Amplified Bible says:

Therefore be imitators of God [copy Him *and* follow His example], as well-beloved children [imitate their father].

Study the nature and character of our Father God, then act just like Him!

First Timothy 4:7 tells us to exercise ourselves unto godliness. The Greek word for "exercise" means *to exercise naked*. In other words, this is telling us that godliness should be our clothing—nothing covering it up. It shouldn't be covered up with facades or phony religious jargon. Godliness is pure and holy just like God. Let's clothe ourselves with godliness.

First Peter 1:16 reiterates this when it tells us to be holy just like God is holy. Holiness and godliness go hand in hand. In 2 Peter 3:11, we are told that holiness and godliness should govern our behavior. First Thessalonians 4:7 says, *"For God hath not called us unto uncleanness, but unto holiness."*

Listen, acting godly and holy doesn't mean that we put on some pseudo-religious face and act solemn all the time. Actually, just the opposite is true. If we add godliness to our lives, then we are going to utilize the fruit that the Spirit of Holiness has put in us. We're going to walk in love, be joyous, remain in peace, stay steadfast, treat people with kindness, allow goodness to lead us, exercise faith and faithfulness, display meekness and humility, and execute self-control. A person who walks like that is one who is good, stable, fun, happy, kind, peaceful, honest, loveable, faithful, and humble. *That* is the way a person is when they are truly holy and godly.

Let's *add godliness* to our lives!

CHAPTER EIGHT

BROTHERLY KINDNESS

Let me reiterate the assistants we've studied so far. The first assistant is *virtue*. Virtue means modesty, purity, and moral excellence with regards to our thoughts, feelings, and actions. The second assistant is *knowledge*. Knowledge means a close, intimate understanding of God that comes by spending time in prayer and the study of His Word on a regular basis. The third assistant is *temperance*. Temperance means mastering our desires and passions, especially our sensual appetites—which really means, self-control. The fourth assistant is *patience*. Patience means endurance, perseverance, and steadfastness. The fifth assistant is *godliness*. Godliness means to be reverent and respectful. Simply put, it means that we are to act like God would act and talk like God would talk in any given situation.

Now, let's go on to the sixth assistant mentioned in Second Peter, chapter one. Verse seven lists the next assistant as *brotherly kindness*. The Greek word translated as *brotherly kindness* is **philadelphia**. It refers to the love that we should have for one another as brothers and sisters in Christ. Christians should be kind to one another. Listen, this is so important that God said we need to add this to our faith. In fact, He said this is one of the things that will keep us from falling!

Look at Ephesians 4:32.

Be ye kind one to another, tenderhearted, forgiving one another, even as God for Christ's sake hath forgiven you.

It is interesting that God has to tell us, His body, to be nice to each other. That implies that there are Christians not being nice to each other. Notice that it doesn't say be nice just to the Christians that are nice to you, or be nice to them if they believe the way you do, or be nice to them unless they've fallen into sin. Our love for other believers is not based on what they do or don't do, or what they've done or not done! This verse says "be kind"—period!

Listen friends, an act of kindness to a brother or sister may be the very thing they need to lift them up and out of the mess they are in. There are too many Christians, preachers included, who are not kind to each other. Just because a brother or sister does something that we don't agree with, doesn't give us the right to shun them or treat them unkindly.

Look at Romans 12:10. It says, "*Be kindly affectioned one to another with brotherly love; in honor preferring one another.*" The words "brotherly love" come from the same Greek word **philadelphia** as do the words *brotherly kindness* from our study text. This is a virtue that we need to exercise in our lives in order to be strong and stable Christians.

Let's take a closer look at what the Holy Ghost said through the Apostle Paul here in Roman 12:10. God told us to be "kindly affectioned one to another." The Greek word used here speaks of the tender love that is displayed between parents and their children, or a husband and wife. It also means to *love tenderly* and *to cherish*. If one of our kids or our spouse treats us wrong, do we shun them? Do we cancel appointments with them and tell them we don't want to talk with them or fellowship with them? God forbid! God tells us in this verse that we are to treat our brothers and sisters in Christ with the same mercy, love, forgiveness, and kindness that we would show our immediate family. Now listen, that takes some growing up. It takes some maturity on our part. But it is absolutely necessary if we want to avoid falling into the traps and snares that our enemy has laid out for us.

This verse in Romans goes on to say that we are to honor and prefer one another. When we honor each other and give preferential treatment to one another, the virtue of kindness will be operating in our lives. The world (those outside of Christ) should see us acting like that toward one another. Even though we make mistakes or have different opinions and ideas, they should see us exercising brotherly kindness. That will give them a glimpse of the "Real Jesus." After all, He is walking the earth today—through us, His Body.

When we exercise true brotherly kindness, we will be the light of the world and the salt of the earth that is so desperately needed in this messed up world.

Add brotherly kindness to your faith today!

CHAPTER NINE

Love

Now let's look at the seventh assistant. Second Peter 1:7 says, *"And to godliness brotherly kindness; and to brotherly kindness charity."*

The seventh assistant that is mentioned is *charity*. In Greek, this is the noun *agape,* which comes from the Greek verb *agapao. Agape* means *love, affection, and good will.* Certain translators keyed in on the *"good will"* part of the definition, and thus translated the word as *"charity"*. Even though the word is often used in this way, the word *agape* goes much deeper than just meaning being charitable.

To better understand the word *agape,* we can take a look at how it is used in I Corinthians 13:4-8. The King James Version translates the word *agape* as *"charity"*. So, I'm going to take the liberty of quoting those five verses, using the word *"love"* instead of *"charity"*.

Remember, this *agape* needs to be added to our lives

if we want to stand strong, and keep from falling. As you read this passage of Scripture, determine in your heart that you are going to be a doer of the Word, not just a hearer.

First Corinthians 13:4-8 says:

Love suffereth long, and is kind; love envieth not; love vaunteth not itself, is not puffed up, doth not behave itself unseemly, seeketh not her own, is not easily provoked, thinketh no evil; rejoiceth not in iniquity, but rejoiceth in the truth; beareth all things, believeth all things, hopeth all things, endureth all things. Love never faileth.

In order to bring more clarity to this passage of Scripture, I'm going to paraphrase it using the Greek definitions of the different words. I believe this will really help us understand what *agape* is all about. So, here is my paraphrase of I Corinthians 13:4-8.

Love perseveres patiently and bravely while enduring troubles and misfortunes. Love is always kind and gentle. Love gives no place for jealousy or envy to boil, nor anger to become heated. Love does not glorify self and is not boastful, conceited, or arrogant.

Love is not rude or ill-mannered, nor does it act inappropriately. Love is not selfish, does not demand its own way, and does not put itself before others. Love is not irritable, touchy, or easily upset. Love does not meditate on, keep a record of, or pass judgment because of the wrongs that are done to it.

Love does not thrive upon nor delight in unrighteous or unfair activities, but always congratulates and shares in the joy of those who allow God's truth to be their guide.

Love conceals the faults and errors of others, to protect and preserve them. Love gives everyone the benefit of the doubt, and trusts God to bring out the best in them. Love retains its joy and full confidence in the midst of everything. Love does not back down or let go, but holds fast and remains strong through every situation.

Love is an eternal force that never perishes, never loses, and never falls from its place of power and effectiveness!

Friends, those five paraphrased verses are what true, genuine *agape* love is all about. That kind of love is what God is telling us to add to our lives in 2 Peter 1:7.

It will greatly behoove every one of us to meditate upon and then employ the things that are revealed above. In fact, it is one of the prerequisites for us to keep from falling into the snares and traps of the evil one. Remember, God has put His love in us, giving us the ability to operate in this kind of love. That means we are not on our own! As long as we are doers of His Word, He will back us up with His ability—and KEEP US FROM FALLING!

CHAPTER TEN

DON'T STAY DOWN—GET UP!

In the remaining chapters, I want to cover some very important issues regarding things that we can do to ensure that we have strong, stable lives—lives that will not *fall* apart! But, before I continue, it seems good to me and the Holy Ghost to once again list the seven things that God told us to do. Now remember as you read these things, make a decision to apply them to your life. Being a *doer* of these things is a prerequisite to keep us from falling into the snares and traps of the evil one. Here is our main text from 2 Peter 1:5-8, and verse 10 (with the seven things underlined for emphasis).

> **And beside this, giving all diligence, add to your faith <u>virtue</u>; and to virtue <u>knowledge</u>; and to knowledge <u>temperance</u>; and to temperance <u>patience</u>; and to patience <u>godliness</u>; and to godliness <u>brotherly kindness</u>; and to brotherly kindness <u>charity</u>. ⁸For if <u>these things</u> be in you, and abound, they make you that you shall neither be barren nor unfruitful in the knowledge of our**

Lord Jesus Christ…<u>if ye do these things, ye shall never fall</u>.

Remember, these seven things are "assistants" to our faith. Faith alone will not keep us from falling. We need these assistants working in our lives as well. I'm going to paraphrase the above passage of Scripture, using the Greek definitions for each of the seven things that we have studied. I believe it will further solidify these things in your heart. Here is my paraphrase of 2 Peter 1:5-8, 10:

However, if you want to experience all of these promises, you must earnestly strive (with haste) to furnish your faith with seven assistants. You must first of all put your thoughts, feelings, and actions on a course of moral excellence. That is, you have to train yourself to think, feel, and act according to the highest moral standards and the purest motives, and do everything with integrity and humility. You must also dig deeper to have an intimate, personal, and thorough knowledge of God's Word. Moreover, you must exercise self control by being the master over your senses and fleshly desires. Then, you must stand strong in the midst of adversity. That is, you must endure, persevere, and be faithful, not allowing tests, trials, problems, or persecutions to force you away from your faith in God and His Word. Next, you must show reverence and respect to the things of God, being totally devoted to God and His ways. In addition, you must exercise God's love toward your brothers and sisters in Christ. You must be kind, loving and compassionate toward them—treating them just like you would treat Jesus! And finally, you must employ God's love at all times, being affectionate, charitable and loving to others, the way God is to you. If these seven things are in you abundantly and increasing in you, they will furnish you with everything you need to be active and effective with the knowledge you have of our Lord Jesus Christ... If the fruits of these things are evident in your life, then you will never stumble, fall, be miserable, or enter into error.

Since God said we can add these seven things to our faith—then we can! I don't know about you, but I'm making a decision right now that the next year is going to be the best year of my life. Just think, we can be so stable, strong, and constant that nothing can hold us back, knock us down, or trip us up. We will run the race that is set before us—and we will run to win! It truly will be the best year of our lives!

What if I Do Fall?

I'm not so naive as to think that nobody in the body of Christ is going to fall. I know that we have an enemy who wants to steal, kill, and destroy and there are Christians who have fallen because of his attacks. So, what do we do if we fall?

Let's look at Scripture and receive some wisdom. Proverbs 24:16 says, *"For a just man falls seven times, and riseth up again."* The Message Bible reads, *"No matter how many times you trip them up, God-loyal people don't stay down long; Soon they're up on their feet, while the wicked end up flat on their faces."*

Listen, don't let the devil or people condemn you because you've taken a fall or had a faith failure. Just get up, put it under the blood, and purpose to be stronger in the future! Do you remember what Peter said in his first letter? In First Peter, chapter one, he told us that when we use our faith through tests and trials, it is refined just like gold when it goes through the fire. When gold comes out of the fire, it is purer and more valuable. Likewise, as we exercise our faith through the troubles and temptations of life, our faith will be refined and purified, and we will come out stronger and better than before. That's when God can take what the devil meant for bad and turn it for good!

Even if we do fall, that doesn't mean we are failures. If we fall, God just told us to simply get up again and keep going. The only way we can be a failure is if we quit! So if you've fallen, I don't care if it's seven times in a day, just get up and say, "Devil, I am a righteous person. You can't keep me down. I'll always rise up again. I'm the head, not the tail. I'm above, not beneath. No weapon formed against me can prosper. The Greater One lives in me, and I can do all things because of His strength."

Keeping the Right Company

Now, it's very important to surround yourself with God-loyal people. First of all, you can't walk a victorious life as a loner. Notice what Ecclesiastes 4:9-10 says:

Two are better than one; because they have a good reward for their labour. For if they <u>fall</u>, the one will lift up his fellow: but woe to him that is alone when he falleth; for he has not another to help him up.

We need each other! We have not been called to be loners—spiritual hobos! Notice the above verse says that if we fall, we should have someone who wants to *lift us up,* not make fun of us, laugh at us, belittle us, or condemn us. We need to choose our friends wisely. We should surround ourselves with friends who will forgive us, pray for us, encourage us, and help us.

You don't need pessimistic people in your inner circle, and you definitely don't want a *doubting Thomas* there. Now God may use you regularly to help those kinds of people, but He wants you to continually be influenced by people who speak the Word of God and walk in the Spirit.

Jesus told us how important it is to watch who we follow. Look at Luke 6:39:

And he spake a parable unto them, Can the blind lead the blind? shall they not both <u>fall</u> into the ditch?

Hanging around the wrong people will not keep you from falling—it will actually cause you to fall more often. Look at what the Holy Ghost said through the Apostle Peter in 2 Peter 3:17.

Ye therefore, beloved, seeing ye know these things before, beware lest you also, being led away with the error of the wicked, <u>fall</u> from your own steadfastness.

Notice, the verse tells us to *beware.* That means to be on your guard and avoid. Avoid what? Following the *error of the wicked.* The word "wicked" does not just mean ungodly people. It also refers to people who are not following the law of the spirit of life in Christ Jesus, and those who are more interested in gratifying their own lusts and desires. They don't guard what they watch on television, at the movies or on the computer screen, or where they go, what they drink, etc.

Notice it says, "beware lest you also being <u>led</u> away." People may try to *lead* you to do things with them that you know are not right. You had better watch out! This verse warns that following their lifestyle will cause you to fall.

It is vitally important for you to connect with the right friend and with a man or woman of God who can mentor or disciple you. Find one or more persons to whom you can submit yourself. It should be someone who is sold out to God. It must be someone who encourages you, strengthens you, helps you, and lifts you up if you do fall.

If we associate with the wrong people, then we will "fall" from a position of being steadfast. If you're going to live a life that is strong and stable, you have to remain steadfast. So, choose your friends wisely and choose carefully those to whom you listen to on a regular basis. Having the right people around you can make all the difference!

CHAPTER ELEVEN

TAKING INVENTORY

Let's discuss what we can do to "take inventory" of our lives, so that we don't fall.

Look at 1 Corinthians 10:12-13:

Wherefore let him that thinketh he standeth take heed lest he fall. There hath no temptation taken you but such as is common to man: but God is faithful, who will not suffer you to be tempted above that you are able; but will with the temptation also make a way to escape, that you may be able to bear it.

The Greek word used for "take heed" means *to consider, contemplate, weigh carefully, examine.* God is telling us to examine ourselves and to consider the things that He's talking about. His purpose in telling us to weigh carefully what He says is to ensure that we don't fall. He says (at the end of verse twelve) *"take heed lest he fall."* It sounds like God is trying to keep us from falling! Therefore it would behoove us to *take inventory* of our lives—it could save us from many problems!

If you read the twelfth and thirteenth verses in context, you'll discover that God is trying to keep us from falling into the same pitfalls as the children of Israel. In the thirteenth verse, He tells us that the trials and temptations that we will face are *"common to man."* Our problems are not unique, isolated cases. Stated plainly, you are not the only one going through what you're going through. God said your situation is *"common to man."* It's nothing new!

But God didn't stop there. Notice, the verse keeps going. After God says that our problems are no different than what many others have gone through, He says, *"but God is faithful and will not allow you to be tempted above that you are able, but will...also make a way to escape, that you may be able to bear it."* In other words, we can count on God's faithfulness! He will not allow us to face any situation that we are not able to handle and will also give us the ability to escape its clutches. That means we can handle anything that comes our way!

Let me paraphrase (I Corinthians 10:12-13) so that you can get a real understanding of what it is teaching us.

Pay attention to the mistakes of others, so that you don't make the same mistakes and end up falling like they did. Every problem that you have ever faced, or will ever face, is nothing new. Many others have already gone through the same difficulties. When you trust God, no matter what hardship you are facing, He will be faithful to help you. He will never allow you to go through something that you cannot handle, and He will always make a way for you to escape. Consequently, you won't fall prey to the tests and trials of life; instead, you will be able to handle anything and everything that comes your way, and emerge victorious!

I take great encouragement from the phrase in the twelfth verse that says "take heed lest he fall." That means if we pay attention and believe what God says, we don't have to fall—EVER!

CHAPTER TWELVE

GOD'S WAY: A FOOL-PROOF WAY

Before we finish this teaching on how to never fall again in your life, let's look at one more passage of Scripture. The verses you are getting ready to read will show you a fool-proof way to keep your life from EVER falling apart.

Look at Matthew 7:24-27.

Therefore whosoever hears these sayings of mine, and does them, I will liken him unto a wise man, which built his house upon a rock: And the rain descended, and the floods came, and the winds blew, and beat upon that house; and it <u>fell not</u>: for it was founded upon a rock. And every one that hears these sayings of mine, and does not do them, shall be likened unto a foolish man, which built his house upon the sand: And the rain descended, and the floods

came, and the winds blew, and beat upon that house; and <u>it fell</u>: and great was the fall of it.

Did you see your name in that verse? Yes, it's there! The word "whosoever" in verse twenty four and the words "every one" in verse twenty six, include you and me! Therefore, God is talking to all of us.

In essence, He is telling us that we get to choose whether or not we fall. God said we can either be a *wise man* or a *foolish man*. The wise man is the one whose life stood strong through all the adversities of life, while the foolish man succumbed to all of the pressures that life threw his way, and thus his life fell apart.

I want you to notice that both men faced the same rain, floods, and winds. These things represent the tests, trials, and hardships that we all have to face in this life. Also, notice that both men heard the same Word of God (see verses twenty four and twenty six). So, what made the difference in these two men's lives?

The wise man chose to *do the Word that he heard.*

When things got rough, he didn't quit. Even though it may have looked like the Word wasn't working, he kept doing it anyway. He did it until it worked!

The foolish man heard the same Word, but chose to *not do the Word that he heard.* When things got rough, he may have stood for a little while, trying the Word, but when things didn't change, he gave up. And that's when his life fell apart! According to the "parable of the sower" (Mark 4:17), he was not rooted in the Word.

Notice how it all worked out in the two men's lives.

Being a doer of the Word caused a supernatural foundation to be built in the wise man's life. It was an unseen *rock* that kept him steady and strong through all of the tests and trials. On the other hand, being a hearer but not a doer of the Word caused a weak and shaky foundation to be built in the foolish man's life. It was like unseen *sand* that kept him unstable and weak through all of the tests and trials. Eventually, the weak foundation in his life caused his life to fall apart.

Let's choose to be doers of God's Word—right in the middle of the storms. That will cause us to walk in wisdom, keep our foundations strong, and prevent our lives from falling apart. Think about this:

The problems of life are *no respecter of persons,* and the Word of God is *no respecter of persons.*

The problems are *common to man,* and the Word of God is *the answer for man's problems.*

The problems are designed to *make you fall,* and the Word of God is designed to *keep you from falling!*

Remember, Jude, verse 24, says that God is able to *keep us from falling.* When we do our part, God always does His!

When You've Done All—
Keep Standing!

Ephesians 6:10-17 tells us to be strong in the Lord and the power of His might, and then tells us about the supernatural armor with which He has equipped us. God didn't tell us in that passage that when we've done all to stand—go ahead and fall. No! He told us to keep standing. In essence, He told us that when the going gets rough, we must realize that we have supernatural weapons and armor and that if we'll use them, we won't fall!

Don't try to be strong in yourself. Be strong in the Lord! Use your faith and "put on" the armor. You have a shield that will stop every attack of the enemy and a sword that will put him on the run!

Now that you have read this book and have seen what God has to say, you know you don't have to succumb to the adversities of life that are designed to trip you up and make you fall.

God told us in 2 Peter chapter one that He has already given us everything we need to partake of His divine nature and blessings. He then listed seven things and told us to add them to our faith.

Let me close by once again reminding you of those seven things. This is my paraphrase of what the Holy Spirit said through the Apostle Peter.

However, if you want to experience all of these promises, you must earnestly strive (with haste) to furnish your faith with seven assistants. You must first of all put your thoughts, feelings, and actions on a course of moral excellence. That is, you have to train yourself to think, feel, and act according to the highest moral standards and the purest motives, and do everything with integrity and humility. You must also dig deeper to have an intimate, personal, and thorough knowledge of God's Word. Moreover, you must exercise self control by being the master over your senses and fleshly desires. Then, you must stand strong in the midst of adversity. That is, you must endure, persevere, and be faithful, not allowing tests, trials, problems, or persecutions to force you away from your faith in God and His Word. Next, you must show reverence and respect to the things of God, being totally devoted to God and His ways. In addition, you must exercise God's love toward your brothers and sisters in Christ. You must be kind, loving and compassionate toward them—treating them just like you would treat Jesus! And finally, you must employ God's love at all times, being affectionate, charitable, and loving to others, the way God is to you. If these seven things are in you abundantly and increasing in you, they will furnish you with everything you need to be active and effective with the knowledge you have of our Lord Jesus Christ...If the fruits of these things are evident in your life, then you will never stumble, fall, be miserable, or enter into error.

REFERENCES

1. James Strong, Strong's Exhaustive Concordance of the Bible (New York: Henrickson Publishers, Inc., 1996).

I HAVE FINISHED THIS BOOK— NOW WHAT?

For further feeding, more revelation and increased strength, we offer three other resources. Our book, *Internal Affairs* will help you gain more understanding about using your faith to overcome the problems of life. If you don't overcome them, they will overcome you, and that will not assist your faith!

Our Scripture CD, *Power Up*, will empower you on a daily basis to live victoriously. It is daily bread that is full of faith, victory and power, and will give you the energy and strength that you need to be a winner every day.

Finally, we strongly recommend our Scripture CD's *Heaven's Wisdom Food*. It has been said that a proverb a day will keep the doctor away. Well, I don't know about that, but I do know that God said, *"Wisdom is the principal thing; therefore get wisdom* (Proverbs 4:7). *Wisdom Scriptures* is our 4-CD collection of the entire book of Proverbs. It will fill your life with wisdom and open the doorway for all of God's blessings to come into your life. All of our Scripture CD's (which have no preaching, just scriptures being quoted from multiple translations over a musical background) are available through our website at:

www.larryhutton.org

To Contact
Larry Hutton Ministries
Write:

Larry Hutton Ministries
P.O. Box 822
Broken Arrow, OK 74013-0822

Or use one of the following methods:
Phone: (918) 259-3077
Fax: (918) 259-3158

E-mail: admin@lhm.net
Website: www.larryhutton.org

*Please include your prayer requests
and comments when you contact us.*

VERY IMPORTANT MESSAGE

God wants a personal relationship with every person in the world, including you! God is not mad at you, and He is not counting up all of your sins and holding them against you. He sent Jesus Christ to shed His blood, die on the cross, and then be raised from the dead. And He did all that just so that you can be freed from the bondage of sin and enter into eternal life with a loving Heavenly Father.

If you have never accepted Jesus Christ as your personal Lord and Savior, it is very simple to do. The Bible states in Romans 10:13, "*Whosoever calls on the name of the Lord shall be saved.*" Since it says, "*Whosoever*" then your name is in the Bible! Verses 9 and 10 tell us how easy it is to receive salvation (eternal life). They tell us that if we will say with our mouths that Jesus is our Lord, and believe in our hearts that God raised Him from the dead, we "*shall be saved.*" It is that easy!

If you have never accepted Jesus as your Lord and Savior, then do it today! Say the following prayer out loud—right now:

Dear God, I want to be part of your family. You said in your Holy Word that if I would acknowledge that you raised Jesus from the dead, and that I accept Him as my personal Lord and Savior, I would be saved. So God, I now say that I believe you raised Jesus from the dead and that He is alive and well. I accept Him now as my personal Lord and Savior. I accept my salvation from all sin right now. I am now saved. Jesus is my Lord and Savior. Thank you, God, for forgiving me, saving me and giving me eternal life. Amen!

If you just prayed this prayer for the first time, I welcome you to the family of God! According to the Bible, in John 3:3-6, you are now born-again. Now it is very important, as a newborn child of God, that you get fed the milk of God's Word so that you can grow up in God and become a mature Christian.

If you will take the time to write, fax or e-mail us, we would love to send you some free literature to help you in your new walk with the Lord. We will also be more than happy to help you find a good church that preaches the Word of God—not the traditions of men. This is vitally important for your future success in God.

Finally, come see us sometime. We would love to meet you! Our itinerary is on our website, and if you would like to watch our television program, the information is on our website as well.

God bless you in your journey with the Lord!

OTHER MATERIALS

BY
LARRY HUTTON

<u>Books</u>

➢ God, the Gold, and the Glory:
   Glorifying God through Personal Increase

➢ Internal Affairs:
   Emotional Stability in an Unstable World

➢ Long Life:
   An Assignment from God

➢ What Is The Unpardonable Sin?
   Can A Christian Lose His Salvation?

<u>Teaching CD's - Series</u>

➢ Happy

➢ Heaven's Transfer System

➢ I Believe – Why No Results?

➢ Free From Me

- Just Who Do You Think You Are?
- Did God Do This?
- Healing Made Easy
- Divine Economics:
    Our Covenant of Prosperity
- The Rich Young Ruler:
    The Story You've Never Heard
- Activating God's Power for the Miraculous
- Final Countdown:
    Your Launching Pad to Financial Freedom

Teaching CD's - Singles

- How To Position Yourself For Continual Increase
- Love, Integrity & Excellence
- Faith to be Healed (How to Keep Your Healing)
- No More Blue Mondays
- God's Healing Medicine
- Questions and Answers on Healing
- Redeemed From Sickness
- Don't Quit: Your Miracle is Here!
- Words
- Working for a Living: It's a Trap!

Scripture CD's

➤ Peace Scriptures

➤ In Him

➤ Heaven's Health Food

➤ Heaven's Wealth Food

➤ Power Up

➤ Wisdom Scriptures

Teaching DVD's - Series

➤ How To Improve Your Love Life

➤ Health From Heaven:
  God's Will to Heal All

➤ Just Who Do You Think You Are?

➤ How To Live Free From Every Negative Emotion

Music

➤ Great Peace (Our Latest Instrumental Album)

➤ The Greatest Gift (Larry's Singing Album)

➤ Peace Be Still (Instrumental: Piano & Strings)

➤ Perfect Peace (Instrumental: Piano only)

ABOUT THE AUTHOR

Larry Hutton is a dynamic teacher and preacher for the body of Christ today! He teaches and preaches with a prophetic voice that is changing the lives of multitudes.

Right before he preached his first sermon in 1980, God spoke to Larry in an audible voice and said, "Keep it simple, my Word is simple!" With that mandate from heaven, Larry has become widely acclaimed for the clarity and simplicity with which he teaches God's Word. He believes that the Bible is for us today and that we ought to be able to understand what it is saying so we can apply it and reach our God-given potential. He also believes that we don't have to wait until we get to the "sweet by and by" to enjoy God's blessings. Larry emphasizes that God wants us to enjoy His blessings in the "sweet here and now!" Through plain and practical teaching, Larry shows us what those blessings are, as well as how to receive and enjoy them.

Larry is nationally and internationally known as a speaker, TV host, author, singer, and songwriter. He has become a popular guest speaker at church meetings, seminars, campmeetings, and on Christian television. His teachings about divine healing, prosperity, and victorious

Christian living have challenged and helped many ministers and laymen alike around the world to strive for God's best in their lives.

While his ministry produces a wide variety of audio and video teaching aids, Larry is perhaps best known for his unique and extremely popular series of Scripture CD's, "Peace Scrpitures," "In Him," "Heaven's Health Food," "Heaven's Wealth Food," "Power Up," and "Heaven's Wisdom Food." They feature Larry speaking multiple translations of many verses applicable to the title subject, thereby bringing incredible clarity to the Word. Presented over a soft instrumental background, these unique recordings lend themselves to repeated listening. As a result, thousands of people have been healed, encouraged, and set free by "hearing and hearing" the Word of God as presented on these CD's

If you would like to watch Dr. Hutton's Weekly Broadcast you can find us on Roku, YouTube, Apple, Android, and many other media sources, all the information is available on our website at:

larryhutton.org

Larry, his wife, Liz, and their daughter, Rachel, travel extensively while maintaining the Larry Hutton Ministry headquarters, Television Studios and offices in Broken Arrow, OK.

The Harrison House Vision

Proclaiming the truth and the power

Of the Gospel of Jesus Christ

With excellence;

Challenging Christians to

Live victoriously,

Grow spiritually,

Know God intimately.